Manage Your Time

Ron Fry

KOGAN
PAGE

Other books in this Kogan Page series:
Getting Organised
How to Study
Improve Your Memory
Improve Your Reading
Improve Your Writing
Last Minute Study Tips
Pass Any Test
Take Notes
Use Your Computer

First published in 1994 in the USA by The Career Press,
3 Tice Road, PO Box 687, Franklin Lakes, NJ 07417
This European edition published 1997 by Kogan Page Ltd

Kogan Page Limited
120 Pentonville Road
London N1 9JN

British Library Cataloguing in Publication Data

A CIP record for this book is available from the British Library.

ISBN 0 7494 2353 6

Typeset by Jo Brereton, Primary Focus, Haslington, Cheshire
Printed and bound in Great Britain by Clays Ltd St Ives plc

Contents

- benefits from time management
- put first things first
- gives us control of ur time if u plan ahead u won't be surprised by any new assignment cuz u will b on track with other things
- helps avoid feeling guilty
- u will develop habits that after time will come naturally to u.
- collect my study materials

FOREWORD
A moment of your time, please

[handwritten: b able to plan things ahead, weeks ahead]

All of the titles in my How to Study Programme were originally written, or so I thought at the time, for older secondary school students taking GCSEs, A levels or equivalent. But over the years I have discovered that the students buying these books are either already at college or university (which says wonderful things about the preparation they received at school), are younger secondary (which says something much more positive about their motivation and, probably, eventual success) or returning to further or higher education (about whom more later).

Many of you reading this are adults. Some of you are returning to education; some of you left school a long time ago but have worked out that if you could learn now the study skills your teachers never taught you, you would do better in your careers – especially if you knew how to meet pressing deadlines or remember the key points of a presentation.

All too many of you are parents with the same lament: 'How do I get Johnny to do better in school? He should be getting As but seems to be happy getting Cs.'

I want to briefly take the time to address each one of the audiences for this book and discuss some of the factors relevant to each of you.

If you are a secondary school student

You should be particularly comfortable with the format of the book – its relatively short sentences and paragraphs, occasionally humorous (hopefully) headings and subheadings and the language used. I wrote it with you in mind.

But you should also be uncomfortable with the fact that you are already in the middle of your school years – the period that will drastically affect, one way or the other, all the rest of your education – and you still need to learn how to study! Don't lose another minute. Learning now how to manage your time and your life is key to success now and in the future.

If you are a traditional college or university student (somewhere in the 18—25 age range)

I hope you are tackling one or two of the study skills you failed to master at school. Otherwise, I cannot see how you are ever going to succeed in college. If you are starting from scratch, my advice to you is the same as to the secondary school students reading this book: drop everything and make it your number one priority.

If you are the parent of a student of any age

Your child's school is probably doing little if anything to teach him or her how to study, which means he or she is not learning how to learn. And that means he or she is not learning how to succeed. Time management is arguably one of two of the most basic study skills, the other being reading.

What can parents do? There are probably even more dedicated parents out there than dedicated students. Here are the rules for parents of students of any age:

1 **Set up a homework area**. Free of distraction, well lit, all necessary supplies handy.

2 **Set up a homework routine**. When and where it gets done. Same start time every day.

3 **Set homework priorities**. Make the point that homework is the priority – before going out with friends, watching TV, whatever.

4 **Make reading a habit** – for them, certainly, but also for yourself, if it is not already. Children will inevitably do what you do, not what you say.

5 **Turn off the TV**. Or, at the very least, severely limit the amount of TV watching you do.

6 **Talk to the teachers**. Find out what your children are supposed to be learning.

7 **Encourage and motivate**, but do not nag them to do their homework. It does not work.

8 **Supervise their work**, but do not fall into the trap of doing their homework for them.

9 **Praise them to succeed**, but do not overpraise them for mediocre work.

10 **Convince older students of reality**. Learning and believing that the real world does not care about their marks, but measures them solely by what they know and what they can do is a lesson that will save many tears, including yours.

11 **If you can afford it, get your children a computer** and all the software they can handle. Your children, whatever their age, must master computer technology in order to survive, let alone succeed, in and after school.

The importance of your involvement

Do not for a minute underestimate the importance of your commitment to your child's success: your involvement in your child's education is absolutely essential to his or her eventual success.

So please, take the time to read this book. Learn what your children should be learning. You can help tremendously, even if you were not a brilliant student yourself, even if you never learned good study skills. You can learn now with your child – not only will it help him or her at school, it also will help you on the job, whatever your field.

If you are a non-traditional student

If you are going back to further education at the age of 25, 45, 65 or 85 – you probably need the help in *Manage Your Time*, and the other books in this series, more than anyone. Why? Because the longer you have been out of education, the more likely it is that you do not remember what you have forgotten – and you have forgotten what you are supposed to remember. As much as I emphasise that it is rarely too early to learn good study habits, I must also emphasise that it is never too late.

If you are returning to education and attempting to carry even a partial course load while simultaneously holding down a job, raising a family, or both, there are some particular problems you face that you probably did not the first time you went to school.

Time and money pressures

Let's face it, when all you had to worry about was going to school, it simply had to be easier than going to school, raising a family and working for a living simultaneously. Mastering all of the techniques of time management is even more essential if you are to juggle effectively your many responsibilities to your career, family, clubs, friends, etc, with your commitment to education. Money management may well be another essential skill, how to pay for child care or how to manage all your responsibilities while cutting your hours at work to make time for college.

Self-imposed fears of inadequacy

You may well convince yourself that you are just 'out of practice' with all this college stuff. You do not even remember what to do with a highlighter. While some of this fear is valid, most is not; I suspect what many of you are really fearing is that you are not in that learning 'mentality' any longer, that you do not 'think' the same way.

I think these last fears are groundless. You have been out there thinking and doing for quite a few years, perhaps very successfully, so it is ridiculous to think college or university will be so different. It will not be. Relax. You may have had a series of jobs, brought up a family, saved money, taken on more and more responsibility. Concentrate on how much more qualified you are for further education now than you were then.

Feeling you are out of your element

This is a slightly different fear, the fear that you just do not fit in any more. After all, you are not 18 again, but neither are many of the college students on campus today. Nowadays more college and university students are older than 25 and you will probably feel more in your element now than you did the first time around.

You will see teachers differently and it is doubtful you will have the same awe you did the first time around. At worst, you will consider teachers your equals. At best, you will consider them younger and not necessarily as successful or experienced as you are. In either event, you probably will not be quite as ready to treat your college or university lecturers as if they were akin to God.

There are differences in academic life. It is slower than the 'real' world, and you may well be moving significantly faster than its normal pace. When you were 18, an afternoon without lessons meant meeting your friends. Now it might mean catching up on a week's worth of errands, cleaning your home from top to bottom and/or writing four reports due last week. Despite your own hectic schedule, do not expect college life to accelerate in response. You will have to get used to people and systems with far less interest in speed.

In case you were wondering

Before we get on with all the tips and techniques necessary, let me make an important point about my study books.

First, I believe in gender equality, in writing as well as in life. Unfortunately, I find constructions such as 'he and she', 's/he', 'womyn' and other such stretches to be sometimes painfully awkward. I have therefore attempted to sprinkle pronouns of both genders throughout the text.

Second, you will find many pieces of advice, examples, lists and other words, phrases and sections spread throughout two or more of the books in the How to Study series. Certainly, *How to Study*, which is an overview of all the study skills, necessarily contains (in summarised form) some of each of the other books. But there is some overlap in some of the other books. The repetition is unavoidable. While I suggest you read all the books in the series, they are individual books, and many people only buy one of them. Consequently, I have included in each the pertinent materials for that topic, even if that material is then repeated in a second or even a third book, as these study skills are all interrelated.

That said, I believe the entire How to Study Programme contains a wide-ranging, comprehensive and complete system of studying. I have attempted to create a system that is usable, useful, practical and learnable. One that you can use – whatever your age and whatever your level of achievement – to start doing better at your studies immediately.

INTRODUCTION
Make time to study smarter

John's alarm jolts him awake at 6am.

Because his job keeps him up until midnight on most week-nights, he schedules most of his study time for the mornings. He makes sure he never has a seminar or lecture before 10am.

Unfortunately (for his marks), on most mornings he is so tired, he just automatically hits the snooze alarm and sleeps at least another hour.

On a good morning, he drags himself out of bed and sits down at his desk to study.

Today seems to be a good morning. He is up by 7am, has two cups of coffee, and opens his business ethics book. But John, who recognised long ago that he was not a morning person, finds his attention wandering. All too soon, he ends up resting his head on his book and nodding off... until his flatmate shakes him awake and tells him he is already late for his first lecture.

Maybe it wasn't going to be such a good morning after all.

John's lectures end at 1pm. He treats himself to lunch in the student union building and, afterwards, to an hour of computer games. 'I deserve a break,' he convinces himself. 'This day has been totally frustrating so far.'

Despite his best efforts, he feels guilty anyway, because he is not using his free time to study. By 2.30, with only a few hours left before he has to go to work, he reluctantly turns off the computer. He is falling further behind in his studies every day, so he knows he has to use the rest of the afternoon for reading.

Filled with resolve to catch up on all of his studying before he goes to work, he heads for the library. As he walks, he begins to mentally catalogue the various reading, essays and exam preparation he has to work on. He slows his pace abruptly when it suddenly dawns on him that catching up before the end of the term would require five or six hours of studying... every day... including weekends.

By the time he gets to the library to study, he is discouraged again. Obviously, anything he can do in the next two hours is a tiny drop in the ocean compared to what has to be done. Nevertheless, he resolves to do at least a little bit.

As he pulls out his books, a scrap of paper falls out. It is the piece of paper that he wrote his marketing assignment on two weeks ago… the term essay that is due to be handed in within two days.

Not only has he not started it yet, the textbook he needs is back at his flat. He decides he should run home to get it – the next two hours is the only time he has to work on it before it is due.

On his way home, he meets a friend. The two of them commiserate about their impossible schedules. By the time John finally gets home, he has decided to ask for an extension on his marketing essay. It will be the second extension he has asked for, which means he has now got two overdue essays, one other term essay and four exams to prepare for… in the next two weeks.

There is one hour left. 'How can I do an essay in 60 minutes?' John groans. Deciding he cannot, he throws his bag of books on to his desk and surrenders to the time pressures. There is no way he can get any real studying done in just an hour. He collapses on the sofa, turns on the TV, and asks himself, 'Why is my life so difficult?'

It is just a matter of time

For John, education has become a burden, a time-eating monster that has taken control of his life.

John is not a particularly bad or unusual student. He is not irresponsible or lazy. He really does want to do well, to get good marks, to prepare himself for a successful career. He has just run out of time.

Let's face it, we all experience problems with time. We can't speed it up or slow it down. We need more of it, and don't know where to find it. Then we wonder where it all went.

But time is not really the problem. Time, after all, is the one 'currency' that all people are given in equal supply, every day.

The problem is that most of us simply let too much of it slip through our fingers – because we have never been taught how to manage our time. Our parents never sat us down to give us a little 'facts of time' talk. And time management skills are not part of any standard academic curriculum.

Not knowing how to effectively manage our time, we just continue to use the 'natural' approach.

Just act naturally

The natural approach to time is simply to take things as they come and do what you feel like doing, without schedule or plan. It worked when we were small. It was easy to live from day to day and never really worry about where our time went.

You played when you felt like playing – and you didn't make appointments to play with your friends. There were no deadlines – if your model aeroplane or doll's house didn't get done by the end of the week, no problem. You didn't even own a calendar – if you had a weekly piano lesson, it was your mother's responsibility to remind you to practise, make sure your clothes were clean and drive you to the tutor.

In fact, sometimes there seemed to be too much time – too many hours before school was over... too many days before the summer holidays... too many weeks before your birthday... too many years before you could learn to drive.

Childhood was a simpler time.

Unfortunately for all Peter Pans, there comes a point when the 'take every day as it comes' approach just does not work. For most of us, it is when we start choosing subjects for important exams, such as GCSEs. For others, it may come later with growing responsibilities at college or university.

Why? Because that is when we begin to establish goals that are important to *us*, not just to our parents.

At school, we become more involved in extracurricular activities, such as sport, music or drama, and must schedule practice times, games and meetings, while still fulfilling our lesson obligations and home responsibilities.

In college, we begin thinking about our careers. We choose subjects that will prepare us for that career, may even try to find a part-time job to give us some experience of it.

To achieve our goals, whether it is performing in the annual school musical or becoming an architect, we must commit ourselves to the many and varied steps it takes to get there.

We must plan. We must manage our time.

Whether you are a secondary school student just starting to feel frazzled, a college or university student juggling courses and a part-time job or a parent working, attending classes and bringing up a family, a simple, easy-to-follow system of organisation is crucial to your success. Despite your natural tendency to proclaim that you just do not have the time to spend scheduling, listing and recording, it is also the best way to give yourself more time.

Harder isn t the word I am thinking of

I am sure many of you reading this are struggling with your increasing responsibilities and commitments. Some of you may be so overwhelmed you have just given up. Those of you who have not probably think it is your fault – if you just worked harder, spent more time on your essays and assignments, lived in the library – then everything would work out.

So you resign yourselves to all-night sessions, cramming for exams and forgetting about time-consuming activities like eating and sleeping. Trying to do everything – even when there is too much to do – without acquiring the skills to control your time, is an approach that will surely lead to burn out.

When does it all end?

With lessons, homework, a part-time or full-time job, and all the opportunities for fun and recreation, life as a student can be very busy. But, believe me, it does not suddenly get easier when you leave school or graduate.

Most adults will tell you that it only gets busier. There will always be a boss who expects you to work later, children who need to be fed, clothed and taken to the doctor, hobbies and interests to pursue, community service to become involved in, courses to take, etc.

If you are an adult doing all of this, I am sure I do not have to tell you how important time management is, do I?

There may *not* be enough time for *everything*

When I asked one busy student if she wished she had more time, she joked, 'I'm glad there are only 24 hours in a day. Any more and I wouldn't have an excuse for not getting everything done'.

Let me give you the good news: there is a way that you can accomplish more in less time, one that is a lot more effective than the natural approach – and it does not take more effort. You can plan ahead and make conscious choices about how your time will be spent, and how much time you will spend on each task. You can have more control over your time, rather than always running out of time as you keep trying to do everything.

Now the bad news. The first step towards managing your time should be deciding just what is important... and what is not. Although difficult, sometimes it is necessary for us to recognise that we really cannot do it all and we need to slice from our busy schedules those activities that are not as meaningful to us so that we can devote more energy to those that are.

You may be a long-term Star Trek fan, but is it really the best use of your time to run back to your room to watch all the repeats?

You may love music so much, you want to be in the orchestra, choir and play with your own band at weekends. But is it realistic to commit to all three?

Your job at the local boutique may mean you get 20 per cent off all the clothes you buy. But if you are working there four days a week, have 15 hours of scheduled lessons and are working in the supermarket at weekends, when do you expect to study?

If you are bringing up a family, working part time and trying to attend a part-time degree course yourself, it is probably time to cure yourself of the Superwoman syndrome.

But there *is* enough time to plan

Yet, even after paring down our commitments, most of us are still struggling to get it all done. What with lessons, study time, work obligations, extracurricular activities and social life, it is not easy fitting it all in – even without Star Trek.

The time management plan that I outline in this book is designed particularly for students. Whether you are at secondary school, college or university, a 'traditional' student or one who has chosen to return to education after being out in the real world for a while, you will find that this is a manageable programme that will work for you.

This time management programme allows for flexibility and I encourage you to adapt any of my recommendations to your own unique needs. That means it will work for you whether you are sharing accommodation with flatmates, or living with a partner and children. You can learn how to balance college, work, fun and even family obligations.

The purpose of this book is to help you make choices about what is important to you, set goals for yourself, organise and schedule your time and develop the motivation and self-discipline to follow your schedule and reach those goals.

1 *Take the time to plan*

I recommend that you learn to take care of the minutes,
for the hours will take care of themselves.

LORD CHESTERFIELD

What if you never developed a plan for your school or university curriculum, never even chose specialist subjects? What if you just 'followed your star', wherever it led, taking whatever subjects you felt like, whenever you felt like going to lessons or lectures?

Perhaps you would sit in on a business seminar because you heard Richard Branson made £20 million last year… and went ballooning as often as he wanted.

You have a friend who is studying psychology, so you would go to a psychology lesson with her.

Your father is an engineer and he seems to like his job, so you would throw in a basic science course.

You have just read an interesting feature in the Sunday papers, so you decide to sign up for a journalism course.

And to round off your schedule, you would take any subject that incredibly gorgeous man is doing, wherever it fits!

If you continue like this for three years, you may have broadened your interests and learned a lot (and/or acquired a boyfriend), but you would not have a degree to show for all your work, and you would probably find it very difficult to get a job when you left college – degreeless, remember?

Planning makes the world go round

Consider an even simpler project: try going supermarket shopping without a list. If you are like me and always go food shopping before you have eaten, you will probably end up with a trolley straight out of 'junk-food heaven', full of anything and everything that looks good: pot noodles, crisps, chocolate biscuits and ice cream.

You might run out of money at the cash desk – how could you work out how much money to take if you had no idea what you were buying?

Worst of all, when you got home, you might discover that you already had two packets of biscuits, a freezer full of ice cream and enough crisps for six all-night parties.

But you didn't get cat food (she has been living on tinned tuna fish and muesli for two days) or milk... or anything for tonight's dinner.

Whether your goal is to graduate from university or buy food for the week, the need for a plan should be clear.

Just as clear, unfortunately, is the fact that far too many people do manage their time like the student without a subject or the shopper without a list.

I ve got a secret

Just like the shopping list and the academic curriculum, setting up a plan for managing your time will take effort. But it is an investment of effort that will bring real returns.

Wouldn't it be nice to have some extra time... instead of always running out of it? To feel that you are exerting some control over your schedule, your school or college work, your life... instead of dashing from appointment to appointment, lesson to lesson, assignment to assignment, like a headless chicken?

It can happen.

I will not spend a lot of time trying to convince you that this is a 'fun' idea – getting excited about calendars and 'to do' lists is a bit too much to hope for. You will not wake up one morning and suddenly decide that organising your life is the most enjoyable thing you can think of.

But I suspect you will do it if I can convince you that effective organisation will reward you in some very tangible ways.

Presuming all this is true (and I bet it is), unless you have some very good reasons – a solid idea of some of the benefits effective organisation can bring you – you will probably find it hard to consistently motivate yourself to do it. It has to become a habit, something you do without thinking, but also something you do no matter what.

Yes, I have a few of those good reasons ready to trot out, but before I do so, why don't you spend a few minutes thinking about the potential benefits effective time management might bring you? If you can already spot the potential rewards in your own life, that is even better than waiting for my reasons. Write your ideas in the spaces on the next page, and then see if I thought of anything you didn't in my list below. But don't look at my list first!

Short-term benefits

A time management system that fits your needs can help you get more work done in less time. Whether your priority is more free time than you have now or improved marks, effective time management can help you reach your objective.

1 **It helps you put first things first**. Have you ever spent an evening doing a work assignment for an easy course, only to find that you had not spent enough time studying for a crucial exam in a more difficult one?

   Listing all the tasks you are required to complete and prioritising them ensures that the most important things will always get done – even when you do not get everything done.

2 **It helps you avoid time traps**. Time traps are the unplanned events that pop up, sometimes (it seems) every day. They are the fires you have to put out before you can turn to tasks like studying.

   You may fall into such time traps because they seem urgent… or because they seem fun. Or you may end up spending hours in them… without even realising you are stuck. For example, you waste an hour of study time at the library because you left the required study materials at home, or you sit down in front of the TV to relax while you eat dinner and get hooked watching a two-hour film.

How time management can help me

_____

_____

_____

_____

_____

_____

_____

_____

_____

_____

_____

_____

_____

_____

There is no way to avoid every time trap. But effective time management can help you avoid most of them. Time management is like a fire-prevention approach rather than a fire-fighting one. It allows you to go about your work systematically instead of moving from crisis to crisis or from whim to whim.

3 **It helps you anticipate opportunities**. In addition to helping you balance study time with other time demands, effective time management can help make the time you do spend studying more productive. You will be able to get more done in the same amount of time or (even better) do more work in less time. I am sure you could find some way to spend those extra hours each week.

Imagine that you and another student are working on the same important assignment. You plan out the steps to be completed well in advance and start on them early. The other student delays even thinking about the assignment until a week before it is due to be handed in.

If both of you were unable to find all the materials you needed in the local library, you, who started early, would have the opportunity to send away for them. The student who had only a week left would not have the same luxury, or the same good mark.

4 **It gives you freedom and control**. Contrary to many students' fears, time management is liberating, not restrictive. A certain control over part of your day allows you to be flexible with the rest of your day.

In addition, you will be able to plan more freedom into your schedule. For example, you would know well in advance that you have an exam the day after a friend's party. Instead of having to ring your friend the night of the party with a sob story, you could make sure you allocated enough study time beforehand and go to the party without feeling guilty, without even thinking about the exam.

5 **It helps you avoid time conflicts**. Have you ever lived the following horror story? You finish a seminar at 5.30pm,

remember you have an essay due in the next day, then realise you have no time to do it as you have a music rehearsal at 6pm. Then you remember that your football game is planned for 7pm... just before that evening engagement you organised months ago (which you completely forgot about until you came home and found a not-so-subtle message on your answering machine).

Simply having all of your activities, responsibilities and tasks written down in one place helps ensure that two or three things do not get scheduled at once. If time conflicts do arise, you will notice them well in advance and be able to rearrange things accordingly.

6 **It helps you avoid feeling guilty**. When you know how much studying has to be done and have the time scheduled to do it, you can relax – you know that the work will get done. It is much easier to forget about studying if you have already allotted the time to it. Without a plan to finish the work you are doing, you may feel like it is 'hanging over your head' even when you are not working on it. If you are going to spend time thinking about studying, you might as well just spend the time studying.

Effective time management also helps keep your conscience off your back. When your studying is done, you can really enjoy your free time without feeling guilty because you are not studying.

7 **It helps you evaluate your progress**. If you know where you should be in course readings and assignments, you will never be surprised when deadlines loom. For example, if you have planned out the whole term and know you have to read an average of 75 pages a week to keep up in your business management course, and you only read 60 pages this week, you do not need a calculator to work out that you are slightly behind. So it is easy enough to schedule a little more time to read next week so you can catch up on your schedule.

On the other hand, if you only read when it does not cut into your leisure time (ie, when your assignment does not conflict with your favourite TV programmes) or until you are tired, you will never know whether you are behind or ahead (but I bet you are behind). Then one day you suddenly realise you have to be up to Chapter 7... by lunchtime.

Good time management helps you know where you are and how you are doing... all the way.

8 **It helps you see the big picture**. Effective time management provides you with a bird's-eye view of the term. Instead of being caught off guard when the busy times come, you will be able to plan ahead – weeks ahead – when you have main exams or project assignments due for more than one course.

Why not complete that German literature essay a few days early so it is not in the way when two other essays are due... or when you are trying to get ready for a weekend camping trip? Conflicts can be worked out with fewer problems if you know about them in advance and do something to eliminate them.

9 **It helps you see the bigger picture**. Planning ahead and plotting your course early allows you to see how lessons fit with your overall school and further education career. For example, if you know you have to take chemistry, biology and physics to be eligible for entrance into medical school, and the courses you will take later will build on those, you will at least be able to see why the lessons are required for your A levels, even if you are not particularly fond of one or two of them.

10 **It helps you learn how to study smarter, not harder**. Students sometimes think time management only means reallocating their time – spending the same time studying, the same time in the classroom, the same time partying, just shifting around these time segments so everything is more 'organised'.

This is only partially true – a key part of effective time management is learning how to prioritise tasks. But this simple view ignores one great benefit of taking control of your time: it may be possible you will become so organised, so prioritised, so in control of your time that you can spend less time studying, get better marks and have more time <u>for other things</u> – extracurricular activities, hobbies, a film, whatever.

It is not magic, though it can appear magical.

Long-term benefits

Besides helping you to manage your time right now and reach your immediate study goals, effective time management will bring long-term benefits.

Have you ever sat in a lesson and thought to yourself, 'I can't wait to leave school and forget all this stuff'?

You would not say that about time management skills. They will be useful throughout your life. Preparation is what full-time education is all about – if you spend your time effectively now, you will be better prepared for the future.

Also, the better prepared you are, the more options you will have – effective learning and good marks now will increase your range of choices when you leave. The company you work for or the university you attend will be one you choose, not one whose choice was dictated by your poor past performance.

Learning how to manage your time now will develop habits and skills you can use outside full-time education. It may be difficult for you to develop the habits of effective time man-agement, but do not think you are alone – time management presents just as much of a problem to many parents, teachers and non-students. How many people do you know who never worry about time?

If you learn effective time management skills at school or college, the pay-offs will come throughout your life. Whether you end up running a household or a business, you will have learned skills you will use every day.

Look at the examples of Sam and Chris, both business executives at a large company. Sam has difficulty managing his time; in fact, he often feels controlled by his job. He is always running to get office supplies to complete a report or gets caught in long, unproductive phone conversations with clients, working on the details of some low-prority task or doing work that other people have asked him to do urgently.

The result: a desk always piled high with unfinished (and more important) work. This means he often has to stay late to finish a report or take work home because he just did not have time to finish his presentation or important project when it should have been done – at work.

Chris, on the other hand, makes a list of weekly priorities every Monday and is careful about committing to any projects for which her list clearly shows she does not have the time. Instead of spending all her time putting out fires, handling crises, and doing work that she could delegate to someone else, she refers to her priority list often and always does the most important things first.

She is realistic and knows that she will never be able to do everything she would like. But because she plans, she gets the important projects done… on time. Her boss knows she can rely on Chris to handle extra, emergency assignments.

At the end of the day, Chris usually feels satisfied that she did a good job. At the end of the week, rather than worrying about leftover tasks that need to be tackled on Saturday or Sunday, she can relax and enjoy her weekend.

Her relaxed weekends, in turn, make her even more effective when she returns to work on Monday mornings.

I m not Paul Daniels

Time management is not a magic wand that can be waved to solve problems at school or after graduation. It is not so much a talent as a craft. There is no 'time management gene' that you either have or lack, like the ones that produce brown eyes or black hair.

These techniques are tools that can be used to help you reach your short-term and long-range goals successfully.

The important thing to remember is that you can be a successful time manager and a successful student if you are willing to make the effort to learn and apply the principles in this book.

Spend time to save time

Some people groan aloud when they hear the words 'time management'. They imagine distressingly organised individuals armed with endless lists, charts and graphs, chained to a rigid schedule, with no room (or time) for fun.

If you dislike the idea of being tied to a schedule, if you fear that it would drain all spontaneity and fun from your life, you will be pleasantly surprised when you discover that just the opposite is true.

Most students are relieved and excited when they learn what a liberating tool time management can be.

Let's explode some of the myths that may be holding you back.

Time management myths

Let's look at some fears some of you may have about time management – fears which are groundless.

Save me from my schedule

Inflexibility is most people's biggest fear – 'If I set it all out on a schedule, then I won't be able to be spontaneous and choose what to do with my time later.'

Your time management system can be as flexible as you want. In fact, the best systems act as guides, not some rigid set of 'must do's' and 'can't do's'.

I am captain of the Time Watch

Contrary to common belief, time management skills will not turn you into a study-bound bookworm or time-crunching fanatic. How much time do you need to set aside for studying? Your personal tutor will probably tell you about the 2 : 1 ratio – spend two hours studying for every hour you spend in a lesson.

Rubbish. The amount of study time will vary from individual to individual, depending upon your subject, your abilities, needs and goals.

Scheduling time to study does not mean you have to go from three hours studying a day to eight. In fact, planning out your study time in advance often means you can relax more when you are not studying because you will not be worrying about when you are going to get your homework done – the time has been set aside.

How long you study is less important than how effective you are when you do sit down to study. The goal is not to spend more time studying, but to spend the same or less time, getting more done in whatever time you spend.

It s just too complicated

Many fear that time management implies complexity. Actually, I recommend simplicity. The more complex your system, the harder it will be to use and, consequently, the less likely you are to use it consistently. The more complex the system, the more likely that it will collapse.

It s too inflexible

You can design your time management system to fit your own needs. Some of the skills you will learn in this book will be more helpful to you in reaching your goals than others. You may already be using some of them. Others you will want to start using immediately, while still others may not fit your needs at all.

Use the skills that are most likely to lead you to your study goals, meet your needs and fit with your personality.

For example, two excellent students approach study and time management in nearly opposite ways.

Alison plans out almost every detail of her morning and afternoon, scheduling long blocks of time for study, work and other tasks. On the other hand, she leaves her evenings flexible and, when she goes out, she also leaves her schedule behind.

Tim prefers to work throughout the day, scheduling all of his activities in smaller blocks of time. He could never spend eight hours continuously studying, as Alison often does. He also has smaller blocks of free time scattered throughout the day and evening.

Are you like Tim, or Alison – or a sort of a mix?

It doesn't matter. What does matter is that as long as their systems work for each of them, there is nothing inherently right or wrong, good or bad, about either. They work.

Time management realities

So much for the myths and fears. Let's look at what is actually required to use time management skills effectively.

A good notebook and a sharp pencil

For time management to work, you have to be able to look at your plan when it's time to use it. It is nearly impossible to make detailed plans very far in advance without having a permanent record. Make it your rule – 'If I plan it out, I will write it down'.

Make sure that you have one place to write and keep all your schedule information, including lesson times, meetings, study times, project handing-in dates, holidays, doctor's appointments, social events, etc, so you always know exactly where to find them.

I have provided some schedule formats in Chapter 8 for you to use or adapt. I have found them effective and they will be covered in greater detail in later chapters. There are hundreds of other schedule planners available in bookshops and stationers, but you can create your own in your notebook.

Your readiness to adapt and personalise

The time management system that best suits you will be tailor-made to fit your needs and personality. Many of the approaches included in this book are general suggestions that work well for many people, but that does not mean each one will be right for you.

Consider the following example. While most parents turn the lights out and keep things quiet when their baby is trying to go to sleep, one baby I know, who spent two months in the hustle and bustle of a newborn intensive care unit, could not sleep unless the lights were on and it was noisy.

Similarly, while many students will study best in a quiet environment, others may feel uncomfortable in a 'stuffy' library and prefer studying in their livingroom.

Make your study schedule work for you, not your night-owl roommate who must plan every activity down to the minute. Alter it, modify it, make it stricter, make it more flexible. Whatever works for you.

Regular attention and consistent use

We have all had the experience of missing an important appointment or commitment and saying, 'I know I had that written down somewhere – I wonder where?'

It is easy to think, 'I'll write it down so I will not forget', but a schedule that is not used regularly is not a schedule at all, let alone a safety net. You must consistently write down your commitments. You must spend time filling out your schedule every week, every day.

Any efforts you make to manage your time will be futile if you do not have your schedule with you when you need it. For example, you are in an art lesson without your schedule when your teacher tells you when your next project has to be handed in. You jot it down in your art notebook and promise yourself you will add it to your schedule as soon as you get home.

You hurry to your next lesson, and your geology lecturer schedules a study session for the following week. You scribble a reminder in your lab book.

Between lessons, a friend stops you to invite you to a party on Thursday night. You promise you will be there.

You arrive at work to find out your supervisor has scheduled your hours for the following week. She checks them with you, they seem fine, so you agree to do them.

Had you been carrying your schedule with you, you would have been able to write down your art project and schedule the necessary amount of preparation time.

You would have realised that your geology study session was the same night as your friend's party and discovered that accepting the work schedule your supervisor presented left you with little time to work on your art project.

Take your schedule with you anywhere and everywhere you think you might need it.

When in doubt, take it along!

Keeping your schedule with you will reduce the number of times you have to say, 'I'll just try to remember it for now' or 'I will write it down on this little piece of paper and transfer it to my planner later'.

Always make a point of writing down tasks, assignments, phone numbers and other bits of important information in your schedule immediately.

A trial run

In order to test its effectiveness, you must give any time management system a chance to work – give it a trial run. No programme can work unless it is utilised consistently. And consistency will not happen without effort.

It is just like learning to ride a bicycle. It is a pain at first; you may even fall off a few times. But once you are a two-wheel pro, you can travel much faster and further than you could on foot.

The same goes for the techniques you will learn here – they may take practice and a little getting used to, but once you have lived a 'reorganised' life for a couple of weeks, you will probably find yourself in the habit of doing it. From then on, it will take relatively little effort to maintain.

That is when you will really notice the pay-off – when the task becomes second nature.

3 *Set the stage for success*

Cathy gets home from work and makes herself a sandwich. It has been a long, tiring day. It is after 5pm and she knows she has to start her homework. Sandwich in hand, she clears a spot on the table between the breakfast dishes and gets out her books. She starts to read but finds it difficult to concentrate. She reads off and on as she finishes her sandwich.

'It's the dishes', she concludes, holding the washing-up responsible for diverting her attention from her studies. She decides to take a break to tidy up. Twenty minutes later, Cathy sits down at a clear table.

Five minutes after that, however, her mother arrives home from work and begins preparing dinner. Cathy tries to read as her mother cuts up vegetables and asks Cathy questions about a forthcoming party.

Half an hour later, after they have finished planning a clothes shopping trip, Cathy can see that her study efforts are not working. She clears her books off the table so her mother can lay it for dinner, and vows to stay up past midnight, if necessary, to get her reading done.

It is obvious that, despite Cathy's motivation to study, she seemed to be in the wrong place at the wrong time. That is exactly how many of you probably feel when the elements of your study environment work against you.

What is *your* best study environment?

There is no one right combination of factors that constitutes a perfect study environment for everyone. However, to be effective, you must find the combinations of place and time that work for you.

Of all the suggestions and techniques discussed in this book, careful attention to where and when you study is probably the simplest and easiest to apply. And the right mix will make a big difference in your productivity.

Unlike Cathy, Luke studies at his desk. He keeps all his materials nearby, avoiding needless trips to other rooms of the house.

He keeps the desk itself clear of books and piles of paper so he can spread out his work and study comfortably.

The area is well lit, so he rarely has problems with headaches or eyestrain.

Finally, because he studies in an area removed from the activity of the rest of the house, he is rarely interrupted by others... or distracted by things like the television, telephone or dirty dishes.

Who do you think gets more done in less time?

Where should you study?

▌ **At the library**. There may be numerous choices, from the large reading room, to quieter, sometimes deserted speciality rooms, to your own study cubicle.

▌ **At home**. Remember that this is the place where distractions are most likely to occur. No one tends to telephone you at the library, and little brothers (or your own children) will not find you easily in there. But home is, of course, usually the most convenient place to make your study headquarters. It may not, however, be the most effective.

▌ **At a friend's, neighbour's or relative's**. This may not be an option at all for many of you, even on an occasional basis, but you may still want to set up one or two alternative study sites. Despite many experts' opinion that you must study in the same place every night, I have a friend who simply craves some variety to help motivate him. He has four different places in which he likes to study and simply rotates them from night to night. Do whatever you find works best for you.

▎ In an empty classroom. Certainly an option at many colleges and perhaps some independent schools, it is an interesting idea mainly because so few students have ever thought of it. While not a likely option at a state school, it never hurts to ask if you can make some arrangements. Since many sports teams practise until 6pm or later, there may be a part of the school open – and usable with permission – even if the rest is locked up tight.

▎ At your job. Whether you are a student working part time or a full-time worker going to college part time, you may be able to make arrangements to use an empty office, even during regular office hours, or perhaps after everyone has left (depending on how much your boss trusts you). If you are in secondary school and a parent, friend or relative works nearby, you may be able to work from just after school until closing time at that person's workplace.

A place just for study

Psychologists know that you can often predict human behaviour accurately if you know just one thing: the individual's environment at the time. We are conditioned to behave in certain ways based on specific cues from our environments.

Not only are certain environments cues for specific behaviours, the more we behave a certain way in a given environment, the stronger that tendency becomes. Repetition is the way habits are formed.

For example, what would the environmental cue of a plastic bowl lead a dog to do?

It all depends on what he has done in the past with that bowl. If it is his food dish, getting it out may make his mouth water. But if his owner usually uses it to play catch with him, he may jump about playfully when he sees it.

What about you? What does your pillow suggest to you? 'Sleep' should be your immediate response. So if you study on your bed, propped up by your pillows, you may find yourself falling asleep soon after you open your books. In fact, if you study regularly in bed, you may eventually not be able to sleep well there.

If possible, designate an area in your room or house that is just for studying. You will eventually condition yourself to the extent that just sitting down at your desk will help you gear up for studying.

To get to this point, however, you will have to make sure you do not allow your mind to become conditioned to other things while sitting at your study desk or table. If you feel tired or are finding it difficult to concentrate, don't put your head down on your desk to rest or daydream. If you need a break, get up and rest in an easy chair or on your bed. Or go for a walk.

If you physically get up and leave your study area when you are not studying, you will help strengthen the conditioning message: 'This desk is only for studying'.

Make it pleasant

It helps if you make your desk or study area a positive place to study. For example, to create a motivating atmosphere, you may want to put up pictures of your dream job to help you remember why you are subjecting yourself to these long hours of study and homework.

And don't push yourself to study for unbearable lengths of time. Few things will make you dislike school or college more than studying until you are sick of the subject matter and your head aches.

Take your own stamina into account. Some people can flop down in a chair, open a book and read or study for hours. Others find their mind wandering after an hour or two. The former person does not need a break. The latter, if he or she wants to study effectively after that first hour or two, should schedule short breaks accordingly. Remember: your study plan should be flexible. Adapt it to your needs, strengths and weaknesses.

Avoid distractions

Consider the location of your desk or study area. Is it in a high-traffic area, where family members or flatmates are likely to be walking through, watching TV or eating? Is it by a window where you can be distracted by passers-by or easily daydream because of the wonderful view? The best position for a desk is usually in a quiet, low-traffic area – for example, in a corner or facing a wall. There might not be much of a view, but there will not be so many easy ways to be distracted, either.

Make it convenient

The perfect study environment, an area meeting all of the above criteria, may not be readily accessible to you. A commitment to always study in the library is not realistic if the library is ten miles away and you don't have a car.

If you have a two-hour free period between work and class, but it takes you half an hour to drive home to your study desk, you would do better to find a quiet coffee shop to read a couple of chapters, even if it is not as ideal as your own area.

Your study spot should be accessible and convenient.

Have more than one place

Or perhaps I should say your study spots.

You may be a student who can (or must) study in a variety of locations, depending on the demands of your schedule. You may want to study in a doctor's waiting-room or while you are waiting for an appointment with a professor. Or perhaps in the car while you are waiting to pick up your partner from work or as you take your turn to drive the neighbour's children to school.

Even if you have one main study location, occasional changes may be needed because of circumstances. Your room and its big oak roll-top desk may be your dream study environment, but if you spend a lot of time at college or university – which is a 20-minute drive from home – you will want to find a nice, quiet corner of the library to call your second 'study home'.

Do not disturb

It may help to keep a real or imaginary barrier between you and the outside world while you are studying. Shutting the door to your room helps block out noise and prevents many intrusions. A 'please do not disturb' sign is a good way of telling people you are busy and can help put you in the 'study mood'.

All elements of your study environment

Environment is more than location. Whether you mainly study at school, at home, in the library or in your car, there are other elements of a study environment that can inhibit or facilitate studying.

Do you have a comfortable chair? It should be pleasant to sit in, though perhaps not as relaxing as the livingroom sofa.

What about ventilation and temperature? Does your study spot become stuffy and hot, or so cold you have to wear gloves?

What about keeping the radio or TV on while you are studying? Some people work better with a little music in the background, and literally find it difficult to work when it is too quiet. (Although I don't know anyone who works better with the Rolling Stones at 90 decibels or while watching *Brookside*!)

Before you decide this matter for yourself, you may want to time yourself to see how much you can accomplish without music, then time yourself with music playing. If you feel that music is a positive influence in your study environment, go ahead and play it, but remember that certain types of music are more conducive to studying than others. Familiar tunes, with a steady rhythm, are less distracting than songs with lyrics, a variety of rhythms and, of course, high decibel levels.

Give your studies the time of day

We have talked about the importance of *place* when you study, and that you should create the habit of studying in the same place or places. The same goes for *when* you study. As far as possible, create a routine time of day for your studying. Some experts say that doing the same thing at the same time every day is the most effective way to organise any ongoing task. Some students find it easier to set aside specific blocks of time during the day, every day, in which they plan to study.

No matter who you are, the time of day when you will study is determined by the following factors.

1 **Study when you are at your best**. What is your peak performance period – the time of day you do your best work? This period varies from person to person – you may be dead to the world until noon but able to study well into the night, or up and alert at the crack of dawn but distracted and tired if you try to burn the midnight oil.

   Work out the time of day you find it easiest to concentrate and are able to get the most done and, whenever possible, plan to do your most difficult work then.

   Keep in mind that for most people, there are some times of day when it is particularly difficult to concentrate on anything – right after a big meal, for example, much of your blood goes to your stomach to work on digesting the food. You may find yourself less alert if you try to study then.

2 **Consider your sleep habits**. Habit is a very powerful influence. If you always set your alarm for 7am, you may find that you wake up then even when you forget to set it. If you are used to going to sleep around 11pm, you will undoubtedly become quite tired if you try to stay up studying until 2am, and probably accomplish very little in those three extra hours.

   Although sleep is a physical necessity influenced by biorhythms as well as habitual behaviour, we become conditioned to perform certain activities at certain times of the day.

   It is tempting to take those big blank spots in your late-night or early-morning schedule and plan to study. But if you are used to sleeping at those times, you will probably find it difficult to focus on your studies.

3 **Study when you can**. Although you want to sit down to study when you are mentally most alert, external factors also play a role in deciding when you study. Some students are not able to study consistently in the same study spot, however ideal it might be. It is the same with *when* you study. You may be most alert during the late afternoon, but if you have to work from 1pm–5pm, you are not going to be able to take advantage of that time to study.

Many other factors influence your available study times. Being at your best is a great goal but not always possible: study whenever circumstances allow.

4 **Consider the complexity of the assignment when you allocate time**. The tasks themselves may have a great effect on your schedule. Do not schedule one hour for an 80-page reading assignment when you know you read a page in two minutes… on a good day. You need to ensure your schedule is flexible enough to adapt to the demands of the specific task. Fifteen-minute study unit increments might work well for you most of the time (although I expect half an hour is an ideal unit for most of you, an hour only for those of you who can work that long without a break and who have assignments that normally take that long to complete). On the other hand, you may have no problem at all working on a long project in short bursts, 15 or 20 minutes at a time, without needing to retrace your steps each time you pick it up again.

Collect your study materials

Have you ever sat down to study, only to realise that you needed a calculator from another room? On your way to get it you decide to go through the kitchen and grab a biscuit. Your flatmate is making dinner, and you ask her about her new work placement. After a few minutes of chatting, you see the newspaper on the table and read the headlines. As you go back to your room, you pause in the doorway, wondering, 'Now what did I come in here for again?'

Remember time traps? This is one – not having your materials together, which means you have to spend extra time gathering them. You risk getting sidetracked and losing valuable study time.

You can save large amounts of time simply by keeping your textbooks, pencils and pens, calculator and other necessities within arm's reach.

Some students like to use a ring-binder for all their lesson notes. Lecture notes from each course can be kept together and marked by tabbed card dividers. Holes can be punched in handouts and other papers from the lesson and then kept with the course notes. In addition, term calendars, weekly schedules, phone lists and other necessities can all be kept in one place. Using this method means you only have to carry a single binder, not keep track of several different notebooks or folders.

To make sure your binder does not get too full or bulky from the term's work, you can empty the contents occasionally into file folders marked for each course. You may even want to keep a small file holder near your desk to allow quick access to materials from the term's work.

If these become too full as the course continues and materials accumulate, they can be placed in a larger filing cabinet.

This system will keep your course notes and other useful papers organised and easy to find. As you study from day to day, papers often start stacking up on your desk anyway. Create new folders as necessary to hold them.

There are many different ways you can organise your study space and notebooks. You can buy filing cabinets, stack plastic baskets on your desk, invest in an inexpensive packet of multi-coloured folders, etc. The important thing is to always have everything you need to hand when you are ready to study.

Take it with you

If you study away from your home or room, it is doubly important to have everything you need with you. If you are studying in the library and forget your assignment book, you cannot just run to the next room and get it.

Look over your schedule each morning (we will discuss your daily schedule in detail in Chapter 6) and determine what you will need for the day. If you need to study lecture notes from your business class that day, make sure you pick up your notes that morning – or, as mornings are so hectic, pack your briefcase or book bag the night before.

Don't forget to take your schedule with you. We have already seen how easily assignments get forgotten if they are not written down immediately.

The more the merrier

If you have materials that you often need both at home and at school or college, it is a good idea to keep a duplicate set of these essential items there or in your book bag or briefcase. Or find a locker in the buildings where you spend the most time. It is comforting to know that you will never be without essential supplies… wherever you are studying.

How are you doing?

Sit down at your desk or study area right now and evaluate your own study environment.

1 Do you have one or two special places reserved just for studying? Or do you study wherever seems convenient or available at the time?

2 Is your study area a pleasant place? Would you offer it to a friend as a good place to study? Or do you dread it because it is so depressing?

3 How is the lighting? Is it too dim or too bright? Is the whole desk well lit? Or only portions of it?

4 Are all the materials you need handy? Do you have pens and pencils, some scrap paper, a calculator, a waste bin, as well as other equipment that you might need, such as computer supplies or textbooks?

5 What else do you do here? Do you eat? Sleep? Write letters? Read for pleasure? If you try to study at the same place you sit to listen to your music or chat on the phone, you could find yourself doing one when you think you are doing the other.

6 Is your study area in a high-traffic or low-traffic area? How often are you interrupted by people passing through?

7 Can you close the door to the room to avoid disturbances and outside noise?

8 When do you spend the most time here? At what time of day do you study? Is it when you are at your best, or do you inevitably study when you are tired and less productive?

9 Are your files, folders and other course materials organised and near the work area? Do you have some filing system in place for them? If you wanted to look at your course notes from last month – or last year – could you find them?

Create your ideal environment

On pages 44–45, there is a checklist for you to rate your study environment. If you do not know the answer to one or more of the questions, take the time to experiment.

Many of the items on this chart should be understandable by you now. Why you feel the need for a particular environment is not important. Knowing you have a preference is. The following is what you are trying to assess in each item.

1 If you prefer 'listening' to 'seeing', you will have little problem getting the information you need from classroom lectures and discussions. In fact, you will prefer them to studying your textbooks. (You may have to concentrate on your reading skills and spend more time with your textbooks to offset this tendency. Highlighting your texts may help.)

   If you are more of a 'visual' person, you will probably find it easier reading your textbook and may have to work to improve your classroom concentration. Taking excellent lecture notes that you can read later will probably be important for you.

2 This should tie in with your answer to point 1. The more 'aural' you are, the more you should concentrate on listening. The more 'visual', the better your notes should be for later review.

3 This may make a difference for a number of reasons. You may find it difficult to hear or see from the back of the classroom. You may be shy and want to sit at the front to motivate yourself to participate in discussions. You may find sitting near a window makes you feel a little less claustrophobic; alternatively, you may daydream too much if near a window and should sit as far inside the classroom as possible.

4 Whatever location you find most conducive to study (considering the limitations of your current living situation and schedule) should be where you spend most of your study time.

5 How to organise your time most effectively to cover the material may depend, to a certain extent, on the amount of homework you are burdened with and/or the time of year. You may have one schedule during most of the academic year but have to adapt during exam time, if essays are due, for special projects, etc.

6 To some of you, such preferences may only be a factor on weekends, because your day hours are set – you are in school.

   But if you are in college (or in a sixth form that adopts higher education's 'choose your own courses and times' timetabling), you would want to use this factor in determining when to arrange your lessons.

   If you study best in the morning, for example, try to schedule as many classes as possible in the afternoons (or, at worst, late in the morning). If you study best in the evening, either schedule morning classes and leave your afternoons free for other activities, or schedule them in the afternoons so you can sleep later (and study later the night before).

7 Some of us get irritable if we try to do anything when we are hungry. If you study poorly when your stomach is rumbling, eat something!

8 Most of us grow up automatically studying alone. If we study with a friend, there is often more horseplay than studying. But do not underestimate the positive effect that studying with one or two friends – or even a larger study group – can have on your mastery of work and on your marks. (Study groups are discussed in greater detail at the end of this section.)

9 Just because you perform best under pressure does not mean you should always leave projects, essays and studying for tests until the last minute. It shows if you are well organised, and if an unexpected project is assigned or a surprise test announced, you will not panic.

   If you do not study well under pressure, it certainly does not mean you occasionally will not be required to do so. The better organised you are, the easier it will be for you all the time, but especially when the unexpected arises.

10 As we have discussed, some of you may find it difficult to concentrate without music or some sort of noise. Others could not sit in front of the TV and do anything but breathe and eat.

   Many of you will fall in between – you can read and even take notes to music but need absolute quiet to study for an exam or learn particularly difficult concepts. If you are not sure how you function best, now is the time to find out.

11 Back to organising. Starting and finishing one project before moving on to another does not mean you cannot at least sit down and outline an entire night's study plan before tackling each subject, one at a time. Setting up such a study plan is advised, but it may mean you really cannot move to another project while the one you are now working on is unfinished. Some of you may have no problem working on one project, switching to another when you get stuck or just need a break, then going back to the first.

12 There is nothing particularly wrong with taking a break whenever you feel you need to keep yourself sharp and maximise your quality study time... as long as the breaks are not every five minutes and do not last longer than the study periods. In general, though, try to increase your concentration through practice so that you can go at least an hour before getting up, stretching and having a cup of tea or a snack. Too many projects will require at least that long to 'get into' or organise, and you may find that breaking too frequently will require too much 'review time' when you return to your desk.

Form your own study group

Find a small group of like-minded students – four to six seems to be the best size group – and share notes, question each other, prepare for tests together. To be effective, obviously, the students you pick to be in your study group should share all, or at least most, of your classes.

Search out students who are cleverer than you, but not too much. If they are on a level far beyond your own, you will soon be left behind and be more discouraged than ever. On the other hand, if you choose students who are too far beneath your level, you may enjoy being the 'brains' of the bunch but miss the point of the group – the challenge of other minds to spur you on.

Study groups can be organised in a variety of ways. Each member could be assigned primary responsibility for a single course, including preparing detailed notes from classes, lectures and discussion groups. If supplementary reading is recommended but not required, that person could be responsible for doing this and preparing detailed summaries.

Alternatively, everybody can be responsible for his or her own notes, but the group could act as an *ad hoc* discussion group, refining the understanding of key points, working on problems together, questioning each other, practising for tests, etc.

Even if you find only one or two other students willing to work with you, such cooperation will be invaluable, especially in preparing for major exams.

Tips for forming your own study group

▌ I suggest four students minimum, probably six maximum. You want to ensure everyone gets a chance to participate as much as they want while maximising the collective knowledge and wisdom of the group.

While group members need not be best friends, they should not be overtly hostile to one another. Seek diversity of experience and demand common dedication.

▌ Try to select students who are at least as clever, committed and serious as you. That will encourage you to keep up and challenge you a bit. Avoid a group in which you are the 'star' – at least until you flicker out during the first exam.

▌ There are a number of ways to organise, as briefly discussed above. My suggestion is to assign each course to one student. That student must truly master that assigned course, doing, in addition to the regular assignments, of course, any or all additional reading (recommended by the tutor or not) necessary to achieve that goal, taking outstanding notes, outlining the course (if the group decides that would be helpful), being available for questions about specific topics in classes and preparing various practice tests, mid-terms and finals, as needed, to help test the other students' knowledge.

Needless to say, all of the other students still attend all classes, take their own notes, do their own reading and homework assignments. But the student assigned that course attempts to learn as much as the tutor, to actually be the 'substitute lecturer' of that course in the study group. (So if you are taking five courses, a five-person study group becomes the ideal.)

▌ Make meeting times and assignments formal and rigorous. Consider establishing rigid rules of conduct. For example, miss two meetings, whatever the excuse, and you are out. Better to shake out the non-serious students early. You do not want anyone who is working as little as possible but hoping to take advantage of your hard work.

▪ However you organise, clearly decide early the exact require-
ments and assignments of each student. Again, you never
want the feeling to emerge that one or two of you are trying
to 'jump on the bandwagon' of the others.

Studying with small children

As many more of you are studying while bringing up a family,
I want to give you some ideas that will help you cope with the
Charge of the Preschool Light Brigade.

▪ **Plan activities to keep the children occupied**. The busier
you are at college and/or at work, the more time your children will want to spend with you when you are at home. If
you spend some time with them, it may be easier for them
to play alone, especially if you have created projects they
can work on while you are working on your assignments.

▪ **Make the children part of your study routine**. Children love
routine, so why not include them in yours? If 4–6pm is
always 'Mum's Study Time', they will soon get used to it,
especially if you make spending other time with them a
priority and if you take the time to give them something to
do during those hours. Explaining the importance of what
you are doing – in a way that includes some ultimate benefit
for them – will also motivate them to be part of your 'study
team'.

▪ **Use the television as a babysitter**. While many of you will
have a problem with this – it may be the lesser of two evils.
You can certainly rent (or tape) enough quality films so you
do not have to worry about the children watching thugs
bashing skulls in (or bashing skulls themselves on some
video game system).

▪ **Plan your study accordingly**. Unless you are a 'perfect
parent', all these things will not keep your children from
interrupting every now and then. While you can minimise
such intrusions, it is virtually impossible to eliminate them

entirely. So don't try – plan your schedule to include them. For starters, that means taking more frequent breaks to spend five minutes with your children. They will be more likely to give you the 15 or 20 minutes at a time you need if they get periodic attention themselves. By default, that means avoiding projects that can only be done with an hour of massive concentration – you can only work in 15 or 20 minute bursts.

▌ **Find help**. Spouses can occasionally take the children out for dinner and a film (the children will encourage you to study more if you institute this), relatives can babysit (at their homes) on a rotating basis, playmates can be invited over (allowing you to send your child to their house the next day), you may be able to swap babysitting chores with other parents at school and professional day care may be available at your child's school or in someone's home for a couple of hours a day. Be creative in finding the help you need.

My Ideal Study Environment

How I receive information best:

1 ❑ Orally

❑ Visually

In the classroom, I should:

2 ❑ Concentrate on taking notes

❑ Concentrate on listening

3 ❑ Sit in front

❑ Sit at the back

❑ Sit near window or door

Where I study best:

4 ❑ At home

❑ In the library

❑ Somewhere else

When I study best:

5 ❑ Every night; little on weekends

❑ Mainly on weekends

❑ Spread out over seven days

6 ❑ In the morning

 ❑ Evening

 ❑ Afternoon

7 ❑ Before dinner

 ❑ After dinner

How I study best:

8 ❑ Alone

 ❑ With a friend

 ❑ In a group

9 ❑ Under time pressure

 ❑ Before I know I have to

10 ❑ With music

 ❑ In front of TV

 ❑ In a quiet room

11 ❑ Organising an entire night s studying before I start

 ❑ Tackling and completing one subject at a time

I need to take a break:

12 ❑ Every 30 minutes or so

 ❑ Every hour

 ❑ Every two hours

 ❑ Every _____ hours

4 *Just make yourself try*

Motivation is a key element in any time management programme. Without sufficient motivation and persistence, a schedule is just like a car without an engine. You will not enjoy its leather seats and multi-functional stereo nearly as much if it won't take you where you want to go.

I am on the outside, looking in

Motivators are either intrinsic or extrinsic. What is the difference? You enrol on a voice course. While the hours certainly count towards your successful assessment, you attend the lessons because you love singing and you look forward to completing each assignment, which usually involves singing and taping a solo to be played back in the classroom.

You also have to study biology. You hate the thought of dissecting frogs, and you could not care less whether they have exoskeletons, endoskeletons, hydroskeletons or no skeletons at all, but the course is required.

In the first case, you are motivated by *intrinsic* factors – you are taking the voice course simply because you truly enjoy it.

The second scenario is an example of *extrinsic* motivation. While you have no interest in biology, your reward for taking the course is external – you will have completed a science course.

Ways to motivate yourself

To increase the amount of intrinsic motivation you have for education, begin by taking stock of your personal interests. What areas of life intrigue you? Can you take courses in those subjects? Yes, education is primarily a path that leads you on to other things, but the more interested you are in the path, the more likely you will reach your destination… and enjoy the journey, too.

Extrinsic motivation can help you get through boring or unpleasant tasks that are part of the process of reaching your goals. You may need some external motivation to help you do well in the course and reach the larger goals you have set for yourself. Later in this chapter, we will discuss how to use artificial rewards to give yourself a boost if your motivation flags.

A vivid image of your final goal can be a powerful motivating force. One student thought about what his job as a computer programmer would be like whenever he needed some help getting through lectures. Try imagining what a day in your life will be like five or ten years from now. If you have not the faintest idea, no wonder you are having a hard time motivating yourself to work towards that career as a final goal.

Your ultimate goal, while a valuable force, will not get you up every morning and keep you working for years. You also need intermediate and short-range goals, for example completing a difficult course, getting good A level marks, graduating from university and then moving into your first job.

Create a goal pyramid

One easy way to visualise all your goals – and their relation to each other – is to construct a goal pyramid.

1 Centred at the top of a piece of paper, write down what you hope to ultimately gain from your education. This is your long-range goal and the pinnacle of your pyramid. _Example_: Become a successful advertising copywriter.

2 Below your long-range goal(s), list mid-range milestones or steps that will lead you to your eventual target. For example, if your long-range goal were to become an advertising copywriter, your mid-range goals might include going to college, getting As for all your writing courses, completing all required courses and getting a summer work placement at a major ad agency.

3 Below the mid-range goals, list as many short-range goals as you can – smaller steps that can be completed in a relatively short period of time. For example, if your long-range goal is to become a travel writer for a widely read magazine, your mid-range goal may be to gain a journalism degree. Short-range goals may include writing a travel article to submit to the school magazine, registering for writing courses or getting an excellent grade in a related class.

The goals you set for yourself now should not be written in stone. Change your goal pyramid as you progress through school. You may eventually decide on a different career. Or your mid-range goals may change as you decide on a different path leading to the long-range goal. The short-range goals will undoubtedly change, even daily, often as a matter of course.

The process of creating your own goal pyramid allows you to see how all those little daily and weekly steps you take can lead to your mid-range and long-term goals, and will motivate you to work on your daily and weekly tasks with more energy and enthusiasm.

Make goal setting a part of your life

The development of good study skills is the route to your goals, whatever they are. And no matter how hard you have to work, or how much adversity you have to overcome along the way, the journey will indeed be worth it.

How do you make setting goals a part of your life? Here are some hints that may help.

1 **Be realistic when you set goals**. Do not aim too high or too low and do not be particularly concerned when (not if) you have to make adjustments along the way.

2 **Be realistic about your expectations**. An improved understanding of a subject you have little aptitude for is preferable to getting hopelessly bogged down if total mastery of the subject is impossible.

3 **Do not give up too easily**. You can be overly realistic – too ready to give up just because something is a trifle harder than you would like. Do not aim too high and feel miserable when you do not come close, or aim too low and never achieve your potential – find the path that is right for you.

4 **Concentrate on areas that offer you the best chance for improvement**. Unexpected successes can do wonders for your confidence and might make it possible for you to achieve more than you thought you could even in other areas.

5 **Monitor your achievements and keep resetting your goals**. Daily, weekly, monthly, yearly – ask yourself how you have done and where you would like to go now.

Rewards can keep you going

The way you decide to use a reward system all depends on how much help you need to get motivated to study. As we have observed, tasks that are intrinsically interesting require little outside motivation. However, most work can be spurred on by the promise of small rewards along the way. If the task is especially tedious or difficult, make the rewards more frequent so that motivation does not flag.

As a general rule, the size of the reward should match the difficulty of the task. For an hour of reading, promise yourself a 10-minute walk. For completion of a rough draft for a big assignment, treat yourself to a video.

Success begets success

Students often think they should be able to complete tasks out of sheer will-power. Many fear that if their will-power is not strong enough, offering themselves rewards for something they should be doing anyway will further weaken their resolve.

Rewarding yourself can actually be a way of strengthening your self-discipline. If you consistently set up goals that are unreachable, all you are doing is practising to fail.

On the other hand, attempting to achieve smaller goals and rewarding yourself every time you reach them will build your list of successes. As you work on these study goals – and reach them – you will begin to believe in yourself more and your performance will continue to improve.

Remember, your purpose is not to suffer while you study and there is nothing wrong with making it as enjoyable as possible.

Prizes or penalties?

In trying to motivate yourself, do you tend to use the carrot or the stick? Positive and negative thoughts can both motivate.

The following are examples of negative thoughts that students use to motivate themselves.

1 'If I don't get a good mark in this exam, there goes my first-class degree.'

2 'If I don't finish this assignment, I'll have to miss the party.'

3 'If I fail these A level exams, I won't get into university.'

4 'I'll be forced to redo this year if I don't do well on this course.'

Now here are some examples of positive thoughts that students use to motivate themselves.

1 'For every hour of solid study, I can then listen to two songs on my new CD.'

2 'If I get this essay done early, I will be able to go out on Friday night.'

3 'If I can get an A in this course, I'll reward myself with a weekend away.'

4 'If I do well in my A levels, my chances of a university place are excellent.'

Which do you tend to use to motivate yourself? If you are not sure, try the exercise on the next two pages. On the lines beneath the heading, 'This Year's Successes', on page 52, list as many successes over the past year that you can think of. Examples might be getting a good mark on an assignment or a good overall term mark, playing for the college sports team, landing a part in a play or committing yourself to a fitness routine.

Then, on page 53, beneath the heading, 'This Year's Failures', list as many failures as you can think of. Now ask yourself which list was the easiest to fill out? Look at them again. Which has the most items? Before you did this exercise, which items (positive or negative) did you tend to dwell on the most?

Chances are, many of you found it easier to list your failures than your successes. You may have found there was not enough room for all your failures, while you struggled to list even a few successes.

Turn your failures into successes

Failures are just as valuable experiences as successes – in fact, they may well be more valuable. What was one of the first lessons you learned in life? Not to touch a hot stove? Not to put your cat in the washing machine? Not to leave your talking doll out in the rain? How did you discover these profound truths? Probably the hard way. But you learned from these experiences, these 'failures'. Similarly, you can learn from every failure, and then turn it into a success.

Review your list of failures. Think about what you learned from each experience, then reword it so that it is a success story. For example, suppose one of your recent failures was that you handed in an English essay late, and, as a direct result of your lateness, received a lower mark.

What did this failure teach you? You learned that getting projects done on time is as important as doing them well. You realised that you had to learn to manage your time better, so now you are reading this book and implementing a good time management system. You are now taking control of your life, and have just turned your failure into a success story.

Focusing on the positive helps you feel good about yourself and provides excitement to keep your motivated.

This Year s Successes

_____

_____

_____

_____

_____

_____

_____

_____

_____

_____

_____

_____

_____

_____

_____

This Year s Failures

_____

_____

_____

_____

_____

_____

_____

_____

_____

_____

_____

_____

_____

_____

5 *Get the big picture*

Now you are ready to plan.

We will begin by developing a time management plan for an entire term... before it begins, of course. This term plan will allow you to keep your sights on the 'big picture'. You will see the forest, even when you are surrounded by trees.

By being able to see an overview of your entire term – every major assignment, every exam, every essay, every appointment – you will be less likely to get caught up spending too much time on a lower priority lesson, just because it requires regular formal homework, while at the same time falling behind in a more important one, which only requires reading.

When you can actually see you have an exam in accounting the same week your zoology project is due to be handed in, you can plan ahead and finish the project early. If you decide (for whatever reason) not to do so, at least you will not be caught by surprise when the crunch comes.

Start planning early

For your long-term planning to be effective, however, you must start early. Students who fail to plan before the academic term begins often find themselves wasting time filling in their schedules one event at a time during the term. They may also find themselves feeling disorganised throughout the term. Starting early, on the other hand, increases your ability to follow a systematic plan of attack.

Most college and university students – and some sixth form students – are able to pick and choose courses according to their own schedules, likes, dislikes, goals, etc. The novelty of such freedom should be tempered with the common-sense approach you are trying to develop through reading this book. Here are a few hints to help you along.

▮ Whenever possible, consider each lecturer's reputation as you decide whether to select a particular course (especially if it is an overview or introductory course that is offered in two or three sessions). Word soon gets around as to which lecturers' talks are stimulating and rewarding – an environment in which learning is a joy, even if it is not a subject you like.

▮ Attempt to select lectures so that your schedule is balanced on a weekly and even a daily basis, although this will not always be possible or advisable. (Do not change your degree course just to fit your schedule.) Try to leave an open hour or half-hour between lectures – it is ideal for review, post-class note-taking, quick trips to the library, and so on.

▮ Try to alternate challenging lectures with those that come more easily to you. Studying is a process of positive reinforcement. You will need encouragement along the way.

▮ Avoid late-evening or early-morning lectures, especially if such scheduling provides you with large gaps of non-effective time.

▮ Set a personal study pace and follow it. Place yourself on a study diet, the key rule of which is: do not overeat.

It is all routine

You cannot race off to your ultimate goal until you find out where your starting line is. So the first step necessary to overhaul your current routine is to identify that routine in detail. My suggestion is to chart, in 15-minute slots, how you spend every minute of every day. While a day or two might be sufficient for some of you, I recommend you chart your activities for an entire week, including the weekend.

This is especially important if, like many people, you have huge pockets of time that seem to disappear, but in reality are devoted to things like 'resting' after you wake up, putting on makeup or shaving, reading the paper, waiting for public transport or driving to and from college or work. Could you use an extra hour or two a day, either for studying or for fun? Make better use of such 'dead' time and you will find all the time you need.

For example, learn how to do multiple tasks at the same time. Listen to a book on tape while you are working around the house; practise vocabulary for language studies while you are driving; ask your children, parents or flatmates to test you for an approaching exam while you are washing up, vacuuming or dusting; and always carry your calendar, notebook(s), pens and a textbook with you – you can get a phenomenal amount of reading or studying done while queuing at the bank, in the library, at the supermarket or on a bus or train. The more ready you are to transform 'dead' time into study time, the more ways you will invent for yourself.

Strategy tip: Identify those items on your daily calendar, whatever their priority, that can be completed in 15 minutes or less. These are the ideal tasks to tackle at the launderette, while waiting for a librarian to locate a book you need or while queuing anywhere.

One of the inherent advantages of following a strict schedule is that it saves time just by 'being' – eliminating all that time so many of us waste just sitting down and wondering what we should do next. The more time management becomes a habit, the more automatic such decisions become, and the less time you waste making them.

The other big advantage, of course, is the discipline such a strict schedule demands. Discipline is a wonderful commodity in that the more you are able to discipline any single aspect of your life, the easier it is to discipline all the others. Just ask any writer who has confronted a blank sheet of paper and stared – for hours – blocked by unseen forces. Many will tell you the only way to break free is to continue sitting, day after day, trying again and again, no matter how difficult.

That takes discipline!

Collect what you need

As you begin your planning session, make sure you have all the information and materials you need to make a quality plan. Gather your course syllabuses, work schedule, dates of important family events, holidays or trips, other personal commitments (doctor's appointments, parties, etc); and a calendar of any extracurricular events in which you plan to participate. Keeping track of your day-to-day activities – lessons, appointments, regular daily homework assignments and daily or weekly tests – will be dealt with in the next chapter. For the moment, I want to talk about the projects – termly assignments, theses, studying for mid-term exams and finals, etc – that require completion over a long period of time – weeks, maybe even months.

Creating your project board

There are two excellent tools you can use for your long-term planning. The first is a project board, which you can put on any blank wall or right above your desk. You do not need to construct your own project board, although it is certainly the least expensive alternative. There are ready-made charts for professionals available in a variety of formats for your convenience, including magnetic and erasable. (Once again you are learning something that you can use throughout your entire life: professionals call their project boards 'flowcharts'.) Your local art supplier, stationer or bookshop may have a selection of these, or you could copy the format of the one reproduced on pages 60–61.

How does the project board work? It is just a variation on a typical calendar. You can set it up vertically, with the months running down the left-hand side and the projects across the top. Or you can change it round and have the dates across the top and the projects running vertically (this is the way a lot of the ready-made ones are sold). It all depends on the available space you have on your wall.

The more time you have to complete a project, the easier it is to procrastinate dealing with it, even to put off identifying the steps and working them into your regular schedule. If you find yourself leaving long-term projects to the last week, schedule the projects furthest away – the termly assignment due in three months, the oral exam ten weeks from now – first. Then trick yourself – schedule the completion date at least seven days prior to the actual handing-in date, giving yourself a one-week cushion for life's inevitable surprises. (Then try to forget you have used this trick. Otherwise, you will be like the perennial latecomer who set his watch 15 minutes fast in an effort to get somewhere on time – except he always reminded himself to subtract 15 minutes from the time on his wrist, defeating the whole purpose.)

Using your project board

For each project, there is a key preparatory step before you can use the chart: you have to break down each general assignment into its component parts. So, for example, for an English essay on Macbeth that has been assigned, I have identified the steps as:

1 Finalise topic.
2 Initial library research.
3 Prepare general outline.
4 Detailed library research.
5 Prepare detailed outline.
6 Write first draft.
7 Write second draft.
8 Check spelling and proofread.
9 Get someone else to proofread.
10 Type final draft.
11 Proofread again.
12 Hand it in.

Next to each specific task, I have estimated the time I would expect to spend on it (see page 61).

The other project involves working as a team with other students from your entrepreneurship course to create a hypothetical student business. While the steps are different, you will notice that the concept of breaking the project down into separate and manageable steps and allocating time for each does not change.

However, because time allocation in later steps depends on what assignments you are given by the group, we have had to temporarily place question marks next to some steps. As the details of this project become clearer and specific assignments are made, your project board should be changed to reflect both more details and the specific time required for each step.

You should also include on your project board time for studying for all of your final exams. Cramming for exams does not work very well in the short term and not at all over the long term, so make it a habit to review your notes on each subject on a weekly or monthly basis. You have decided that every Sunday morning is 'review time' and allocated one Sunday a month to review the previous month's work in each subject. This is entered on the board as well.

As a result of this plan, you will notice there is little time allocated to last minute cramming or even studying for a specific exam the week before it is given; just a couple of hours to go over any details you are still a little unsure of or to spend on areas you think will be in the exam. While other students are burning the midnight oil in the library the night before each exam, you are getting a good night's sleep and will enter the exam room refreshed, relaxed and confident.

As a by-product of this study schedule, by following this plan, you will also find that salient facts and ideas will remain with you long after anybody is testing you on them.

Now that you have your project board, what do you do with it? Keep adding any other important projects throughout the term and continue to revise the board according to actual time spent as opposed to time allocated. Getting into this habit will make you more aware of how much time to allocate to future projects and make sure that the more you do so, the more accurate your estimates will be.

Sample Project Board

MONTH/WEEK		PROJECT: STUDENT CORPORATION
1st MONTH	Week 1	Initial group meeting: discuss overall assignment and possible products or services — bring list of three each to meeting (1 hour)
	Week 2	Finalise product or service; finalise organisation of group and long-term responsibilities of each subgroup (3)
	Week 3	Subgroup planning and short-term assignments (2)
	Week 4	Work on individual assignment from subgroup (?)
2nd MONTH	Week 1	Work on individual assignment from subgroup (?)
	Week 2	Work on individual assignment from subgroup (?)
	Week 3	Integrate individual assignment with rest of subgroup (?)
	Week 4	Meet with entire group to integrate plans (?)
3rd MONTH	Week 1	Finalise all-group plan; draft initial report (?)
	Week 2	Type and proof final report (?)
	Week 3	
	Week 4	
	DUE DATE	3rd month/end of week 2

PROJECT: MACBETH TERM ESSAY	REVIEW/EXAM SCHEDULE
Finalise topic (1 hour)	Review prior month s history notes (3)
Initial library research (2)	Review prior month s English notes (2)
General outline (1)	
Detailed library research (3)	Review prior month s science notes (4)
Detailed library research (3)	Review prior month s maths notes (4)
Detailed library research (3)	Review 1st month history notes (3)
Detailed outline (1)	Review 1st month English notes (2)
First draft (4), Additional research (2)	Review 1st month science notes (4)
	Review 1st month maths notes (4)
Second draft, spellcheck, proof (10)	2nd month history notes (3)
Independent proof (1)	2nd month English notes (2)
	2nd month science notes (4)
Type final draft and proof (4)	2nd month maths notes (4)
End of 3rd month	End of 3rd month

Using a term planning calendar

The term planning calendar should be used together with or in place of the project board. An example is on pages 64–65, and a blank form that you could adapt for your own use is on page 83.

To use it with the project board

Start by transferring all the information from the project board to your term planning calendar. Then add your weekly lesson schedule, work schedule, family celebrations, holidays and trips, club meetings and extracurricular activities – everything. The idea is to make sure your calendar has all the scheduling information, while your project board contains just the briefest summary that you can take in at a glance.

Leave your project board on your wall at home; carry your term calendar with you. Whenever new projects, appointments or meetings are scheduled, add them immediately to your calendar. Then transfer the steps involving major projects to your project board.

To use it in place of the project board

Just don't make a project board. Put all the information – including the steps of all your projects and the approximate time you expect each to take – straight on to the calendar.

It is up to you to find out which will work best for you. I prefer using both, for one simple reason: I like to be able to look at the wall and see the entire term at a glance. It is much easier to see how everything fits together than trying to glance at a dozen different weekly calendars or even three monthly ones. It is also difficult to see immediately which steps go with which projects without studying the calendar, although colour coding would solve this problem, whereas the set-up of the project board makes this information easy to find.

Secondary school students may find it quite easy to use only the calendar, as they are usually not subject to quite as many long-term projects as college or university students. But once you are in college, especially if you have more than an average number of essays, reports, projects, etc, you will find the project board a very helpful extra tool.

It may seem a waste of time to have to write all these details on both a project board and term planning calendar but I think you will find the time you save more than makes up for the supposed inconvenience.

Term Planning Calendar

Fill in due dates for assignments and essays, dates of tests/exams, and important non-academic activities and events

Month	MONDAY	TUESDAY	WEDNESDAY	THURSDAY	FRIDAY	SATURDAY	SUNDAY
← Feb	18	19	20 Conference 4–5	21	22	23	24
March	25	26	27	28	1 Afternoon: AAP Meeting	2	3
	4 Sociology Presentation	5	6 Math: Ch 1–3	7	8	9	10
	11	12	13 Math: Ch 4	14	15	16	17 Trip Home

Month: April

MONDAY	TUESDAY	WEDNESDAY	THURSDAY	FRIDAY	SATURDAY	SUNDAY
18	19	20 Maths: Ch 5	21	22	23	24
25	26	27 No Maths due	28	29	30 Trip to Diane's	31 Jim and
1 Biology Lab Journal due	2	3 Maths: Chs 6–8	4	5 Sociology paper due!	6	7
8	9 Last day of class	10	11	12	13 Biology final 3.00pm	14
15 Maths final 2.00pm	16	17	18	19 ☺	20	21

CAMPING!!! ⟵———————⟶

6 *Add the detail*

Your project board now lists the major essays, assignments and exams for an entire term. You have also filled out a term planning calendar, including the details on your project board and other key appointments, assignments and handing-in dates.

Now it is time to become even more organised. The project board and term planning calendar have given you a good start by helping you schedule the whole term. It is time to learn about the tools that will help you organise your days and weeks.

For any time management system to work, it has to be used continually. Make an appointment with yourself at the end of each week – Sunday night is perfect – to sit down and plan for the following week. This may be the best time you spend all week, because you will reap the benefits of it throughout the week and beyond.

Step 1: Make a to do list

First, you must identify everything you need to do this week. Look at your project board and/or term calendar to determine what tasks need to be completed this week for all your major college projects. Add any other tasks that must be done: from sending off a birthday present to your sister to attending your monthly volunteer meeting to completing homework that may have recently been assigned. Once you have created your list, you can move on to the next step, putting your tasks in order of importance.

Step 2: Prioritise your tasks

When you sit down to study without a plan, you just dive into the first project that comes to mind. Of course there is no guarantee that the first thing that comes to mind will be the most important. The point of the weekly priority task sheet is to help you arrange your tasks in order of importance. That way, even if you find yourself without enough time for everything, you can at least finish those assignments that are most important.

First, ask yourself this question, 'If I only got a few things done this week, what would I want them to be?' Mark these high-priority tasks with an 'H'. After you have identified the 'urgent' items, consider those tasks that are least important – items that could wait until the following week to be done, if necessary. You may have tasks that you consider very important, but that do not have to be completed this week. These are low-priority items; mark them with an 'L'.

All other items fit somewhere between the critical tasks and those of low priority. Review the remaining items, and if you are sure that none of them are either 'H' or 'L', mark them with an 'M' (to represent middle priority).

Strategy tip: If you push aside the same low-priority item day after day, week after week, at some point you should just stop and decide whether it is something you need to do at all. This is a strategic way to make a task or problem 'disappear'. In the business world, some managers purposefully avoid confronting a number of problems, waiting to see which will simply solve themselves through benign neglect. If it works in business, it can work for you in school.

A completed priority task sheet is on page 71, and a blank form on page 84.

Step 3: Fill in your daily schedule

Before you start adding essays, projects, homework, study time, etc, to your calendar, fill in the 'knowns' – the time you need to sleep, eat, work, attend lessons. Even if your current routine consists of meals on the run and sleep wherever you find it, build the assumption into your schedule that you are going to get eight hours of sleep and three decent meals a day. You may surprise yourself and find that there is still enough time to do everything you need. (Although all of us probably know someone who sleeps three hours a night, eats only junk and still finds a way to get nothing but As, most experts would argue that regular, healthy eating and a decent sleep schedule are key attributes of any successful study system.)

Now transfer the items on your priority task sheet to your daily schedule forms. (See page 72 for an example of a completed daily schedule, and page 85 for a blank form.) Put in the 'H' items first, followed by the 'M' items. Then, fit in as many of the 'L' items for which you still have room. By following this procedure, you will ensure you give the amount of time needed to your most important priorities. You can devote your most productive study times to your most important tasks, and slot in your lower priorities as they fit.

For example, you have a three-hour block of free time on Wednesday afternoon. So schedule your 'H' priority research gathering for your geography project, and plan to start your history assignment, an 'L' priority, between lunch and your 2pm lesson on Thursday.

Other considerations

Besides the importance of the task and the available time you have to complete it, other factors will determine how you fit your daily schedules together. Some will be beyond your control: work schedules, appointments with lecturers, doctors, etc. But there are plenty of factors you do control, which you should consider as you put together your daily schedules for the week.

Schedule enough time for each task – time to 'warm up' and get the task accomplished, but, particularly when working on long-term projects, not so much time that you 'burn out'. Every individual is different, but most students study best for blocks of one and a half to three hours, depending on the subject.

Do not overdo it. Plan your study time in blocks, breaking up work time with short leisure activities. (It is helpful to add these to your schedule as well.) For example, you have set aside three hours on Wednesday afternoon for that research assignment. Plan a 15-minute walk to the cafeteria somewhere in the middle of that study block. You will find that these breaks help you to think more clearly and creatively when you get back to studying.

Even if you tend to like longer blocks of study time, be careful about scheduling study 'marathons' – a six- or eight-hour stretch rather than a series of two-hour sessions. The longer the period you schedule, the more likely you will have to fight the demons of procrastination. By convincing yourself that you are really studying flat out, you will also find it easier to justify time-wasting distractions, scheduling longer breaks and, before long, giving up before you should.

Use your daily schedule daily

Each night (or in the morning before the day really begins) look at your schedule for the forthcoming day. How much free time is there? Are there 'surprise' tasks that are not on your schedule but need to be? Are there conflicts you were unaware of at the beginning of the week?

If you plan well at the beginning of the week, this should not happen often, but it invariably does. Sometimes you will discover a lesson is cancelled or a meeting postponed, which leaves you with a schedule change. By checking your daily schedule every day – either the night before or first thing in the morning – you will be able to respond to these changes.

How do you know whether to enter an assignment on your daily schedule or put it on the project board first?

If it is a simple task and if it will definitely be accomplished within a week – study for a mid-term test, meet to discuss auditions with the drama group – put it on the appropriate daily schedule sheet(s).

However, if it is a task that is complicated – requiring further breakdown into specific steps and/or one that will require more than a week to complete – it should be 'flow charted' on your project board. Then the individual steps should be added to your daily schedules. (I like to plan everything out the night before. It is a fantastic feeling to wake up and start the day completely organised.)

You will benefit every day

Once you start using your project board, term planning calendar, priority task sheets and daily schedules, you will reap the benefits every day. Throughout the day, you can simply follow your daily schedule.

Anything – even studying – seems less overwhelming when you have it broken into 'bite-size' pieces... and you already know the flavour.

You no longer worry about when you will get that essay written – you have already planned the time.

You will accomplish it all – one step at a time.

As you get used to managing your time, planning well ahead as well as planning your week and even your days, you will quickly discover that you seem to have more time than ever before.

Priority Rating	Scheduled?	**Priority Tasks This Week** Week beginning **28/3** and ending **3/4**
		Sociology Essay
H		— _Library Search_
M		— _Outline_
L		— _Rough Draft_
		Psychology Reading
H		— _Ch 4_
M		— _Ch 5_
M		— _Study for test_

Daily Schedule

date: **30/3**

Assignments Due	Schedule
Sociology Lab work	5
Psychology Ch 4	6
	7
	8
	9 History
To Do/Errands	10 Sociology
Call Eric – 871-4031	11
Books to library	12 Lunch w/ P & S
– Bank	1 Read Ch 5 (Soc)
– Supermarket	2
Drop in to see Alex	3 History lesson
	4 TRAVEL
	5
Homework	6 Psychology homework
1. History Ch 5, 1-9	7 Work on essay
2. Sociology essay	8 ←
(rough draft)	9
	10
	11
	12

7 Help! Tips, tips and more tips

This book has shown you a simple, manageable system for getting more done in the amount of time you have available. It is a system geared for people whose school or college schedules demand a big chunk of time, but who also have other commitments, activities and responsibilities pulling them in other directions.

Your time management plan should be simple. Why agree to do another complicated project that demands your time and mental energies? No matter how basic and easy to use your programme may be, this does not guarantee that you will not be plagued with a time management problem from time to time.

As you try to implement the suggested time management skills in your life, you are bound to have some slip-ups. Learn some problem-solving skills so these study roadblocks do not stop your progress completely.

Hitting the wall

If you come up against a wall on your path to organisational success, the best solution is to find creative ways to get around it, rather than trying to crash your way through it.

For example, if you are trying to lose weight, there are a number of different approaches you could take.

You could try to alter your *behaviour* – eat less, exercise more.

Or change your *attitude* towards eating, maybe stop using food as a reward.

Or transform your *environment*, keeping the 'fridge stocked with only healthy fruits and veg... and moving your study area from the kitchen to the bedroom.

More than likely, your weight loss will result from a combination of changes in all three areas.

Here are several examples of creative and multi-dimensional approaches to solving typical time management problems.

Time flies when you are having fun

And sometimes even when you are not. No matter how hard you try to stick to your schedule, you find your assignments always take a lot longer than planned. You schedule an hour to do your economics homework, and it takes you twice that long. You plan an afternoon at the library for research, and it is closing time before you are ready to leave. It seems you spend all your time studying – and you are still not getting it done.

Solutions: It is time for an attitude check. Are you being too much of a perfectionist? Is it taking you so long to read because you are trying to memorise every word? Make sure your expectations for yourself are realistic. Do not exaggerate the importance of lower priority assignments.

Consider altering your behaviour – with a little help from an alarm clock. If you have planned an hour for your reading assignment, set the clock to go off when you should have completed it. Then, stop reading and go on to the next task. If you have not finished, reassure yourself that you can go back to it later. You will probably become conditioned to complete your assignments more quickly, and you will not run the risk of leaving your other, perhaps more important, work unfinished.

I m allergic to my desk

There is nothing wrong with your study area. It is in a quiet corner of the house with few distractions. All your materials are nearby, and the area is well lit and well ventilated. But… every time you sit down to study, you find yourself coming up with any excuse to leave. Unable to focus on any assignment, your mind wanders off.

Solution: It can happen. You set up the ideal study area, follow your time management system and stick to your schedule religiously. Your intentions are good, but, for some reason, it does not work. Bad vibes, maybe. What can you do?

Change your environment.

Just as you can condition yourself to study, you can also condition yourself not to study in a particular location. Stick to your schedule, but try another area – another floor in the library, or even a place that may not seem to be as conducive to quiet study. Maybe you are one of those people who needs a little music or activity in the background to concentrate.

If changing your environment does not help, consider altering your study routine. Are you trying to study at a time of day when you have far too much pent-up energy? Maybe changing your study time to an earlier or later time would help. Try taking a brisk walk or doing some exercises before you begin studying.

Think about other behaviour: have you had several cups of coffee (or cans of Coke) prior to your study period? Caffeine overdose – or too much sugar and caffeine – can make it very difficult to concentrate.

A conspiracy to keep you from studying

Friends and family visit or phone when you are studying because they know that is the best time to find you at home. Or you are interrupted by phone calls for family members or flatmates. Worse yet are the calls from people taking surveys, asking for donations or trying to sell you something.

Solutions: A ringing phone is virtually impossible to ignore. Even if you are determined not to pick it up, it still demands your attention. An answering-machine will eliminate involvement in lengthy conversations, but your train of thought will still be interrupted.

There are a few environment-altering solutions: unplug the phone or turn down the volume on the bell and let your answering-machine take the calls while you are studying. Or remove yourself from within hearing range – go to the library.

A little help from your friends

Your flatmate, whose study hours differ from yours, always seems to want to spend 'quality bonding time' in the middle of your heavy reading assignments.

Solutions: It is not rude to refuse to talk to someone while you are studying, but it often feels like that, and I would rather feel guilty about not studying than being rude to a friend. A favourite tip from human relations specialists is to respond in a positive but diverting way – eg, 'It sounds like this is important to you. I really want to hear more. Can we talk in an hour when I have finished this, so I can concentrate more on your problem?' (Agreed, your flatmate would look at you as if you were mad if you talked like this. Put it in your own words – it is the attitude that is important.)

Another solution might be to put up a 'Do Not Disturb' sign, indicating the time you will be available to talk. The visual signal helps remind others that you are busy before they unintentionally interrupt you with small talk.

You can t count on anyone

You painstakingly plan your schedule each week, religiously keeping track of each appointment, assignment and commitment you have. Unfortunately, others do not seem to have the same sense of responsibility. Your friends cancel social engagements, you arrive on time for a meeting and no one else in the group shows up, even your teacher postpones the pre-exam study session.

Solution: Yes, it is time for another attitude adjustment. Welcome to the real world.

First of all, there is really nothing you can do when someone else cancels or postpones a scheduled appointment. But if you remember, at the beginning of this book I said that fanaticism is not an element of a good time management programme.

Occasional – and sometimes more than occasional – cancellations, postponements or reschedulings should not ruin your schedule.

Try looking at such last-minute changes as opportunities. Your tutor cancelled your appointment? That means a free hour to practise French vocabulary, read another history chapter, work out at the gym… or just do nothing.

A special note for commuters

If you live at home (as opposed to being housed on campus), there are some special pressures with which you need to contend.

▌ Travelling to college will probably take longer than if you could roll out of bed and walk there. It will require more wakefulness, even if you only have to stumble to a station or bus (but especially if you have to drive). You will also have travel time problems if you need to return to the campus for any reason after you have returned home. It is especially important that you minimise travel time, planning enough to maximise your use of the campus facilities without scheduling a trip home in between.

▌ While nobody likes walking in rain, sleet or snow, it is invariably easier to walk a few tree-lined streets than drive a few miles in inclement weather. Take weather problems into account when planning your journey.

▌ The very act of living at home – whether as a child or one 'married with children' – brings with it responsibilities to others you could minimise by living in at college. Be ready to allocate time to these responsibilities and include them in your study schedule. They are an inevitable part of life if you live at home.

Old habits die hard

As you begin to implement your own organisational system for success, you may need to rid yourself of some old habits.

1 **Do not make your schedule too vague**. When you are scheduling your time, be specific about which tasks you plan to do, and when you plan to do them.

2 **Do not delay your planning**. It is easy to convince yourself that you will plan the details of a particular task when the time comes. But this makes it much too easy to forget your homework when your friends invite you to go to the park or out for a pizza.

3 **Write *everything* down**. Not having to remember all these items will free up space in your brain for the things you need to concentrate on or do have to remember. As a general rule, write down the so-called little things and you will avoid data overload and clutter.

4 **Learn to manage distractions**. 'Don't respond to the urgent and forget the important.' It is easy to become distracted when the phone rings, your baby brother chooses to trash your room or you realise your favourite TV programme is coming on. But do not just drop your books and run off. Take a few seconds to make sure you have reached a logical stopping point and jot down a note to yourself of exactly where you left off and/or anything you want to remember after your break. Then you can enjoy your break.

5 **Do not 'shotgun' plan**. Even if you have not been following a systematic time management approach, you may have had some way of keeping important dates and events in mind. Some students use what might be called the 'shotgun' approach – writing down assignments, dates and times on whatever is available. They end up with so many slips of paper in so many places, their planning attempts are virtually worthless.

   Record all future events and tasks on your project board and/or term planning calendar. Always have your calendar with you so you can refer to it when you are planning a specific week or day or need to add an appointment or assignment to it.

6 **Do not over-schedule**. As you begin to follow a time management programme, you may find yourself trying to schedule too much of your time. Once you get the 'effectiveness bug' and become aware of how much you can accomplish, it might be tempting to squeeze more and more into your life.

7 **Be realistic and honest with yourself** when determining those things that require more effort, those that come easier to you. Chances are you cannot complete the outline for your project assignment, study three chapters of biology and do your French assignment in the two hours you have between lessons and work. Schedule enough time to complete each assignment. Whenever possible, schedule pleasurable activities after study time, not before. They will act as incentives, not distractions.

8 **Remember that time is relative**. Car journeys take longer if you have to schedule frequent stops for petrol, food, necessities, etc, longer still if you start out during rush hour. Similarly, libraries are more crowded at certain times of the day or year, which will affect how quickly you can get books you need. So take the time of day into account.

   If your schedule involves working with others, you need to take their sense of time into account – you may find you have to schedule waiting time for an unpunctual friend, so always have a book with you.

9 **Be prepared**. As assignments are entered on your calendar, make sure you also enter items needed for their completion – texts, other books you have to buy, borrow or get from the library, special materials, etc. There is nothing worse than sitting down to do that assignment you have put off until the last minute and realising that though you are finally ready to get to work, your supplies are not… and at 10pm, you do not have many options.

10 **Be realistic**. Plan according to your schedule, your goals and your aptitudes, not some ephemeral 'standard'. Allocate the time you expect a project to take you, not the time it might take someone else, how long your teacher tells you it should take, etc. There will be tasks you complete far faster than anyone else, and others that take you much longer.

11 **Be flexible, monitor and adjust**. No calendar is an island. Any new assignment will affect whatever you have already scheduled. If you have a reasonably light schedule when a new assignment suddenly appears, it can be slotted into your calendar and finished as scheduled. But if you have already planned virtually every hour for the next two weeks, any addition may force you to change a whole day's plan. Be flexible and be ready. It will happen.

Remember that no plan of action is foolproof, so monitor your progress and make changes where necessary. This is your study regime – you conceived it, you can change it.

12 **Look for more time savings**. If you find that you are consistently allotting more time than necessary to a specific chore – giving yourself one hour to review your English notes every Sunday but always finishing in 45 minutes or less – change your future schedule accordingly.

13 **Accomplish one task before going on to the next one** – do not skip around.

14 **Do your least favourite chores** (study assignments, projects, whatever) first – you will feel better getting them out of the way. Plan how to do them as efficiently as possible, that will get rid of them even faster.

15 **Try anything that works**. You may decide that colour coding your calendar – red for assignments that must be accomplished that week, blue for steps in longer-term projects (which give you more flexibility), yellow for personal time and appointments, green for lessons, etc – makes it easier for you to tell at a glance what you need to do and when you need to do it.

Perhaps you need a day-to-day calendar to carry with you, but a duplicate one on the wall at home.

Once you are used to using your lesson schedule, you may decide to eliminate lesson times from your calendar and make it less complicated.

16 **Adapt these tools to your own use**. Try anything you think may work – use it if it does, discard it if it does not.

There are thinkers and there are doers. And there are those who think a lot about doing.

Organising your life requires you to actually use the project board, term calendar, priority task sheets and daily schedules we have discussed, not just waste more time 'planning' instead of studying.

Planning is an ongoing learning process. Dive in and plan for your next academic term. Or if you are currently in the middle of a term, plan the remainder of it now. As you use your plan in the forthcoming weeks and months, you will come up with new ideas for improving your time management system in the future and tailoring it to your own needs.

As you get used to managing your time, planning ahead as well as planning your week and even your days, you will quickly discover that you seem to have more time than ever before.

8 *Time management forms*

In this chapter I have included blank copies of each of the three key tools introduced in this book: the priority task sheet, daily schedule and term planning calendar forms. Please use as many of these forms as you need, enlarge them to fit in your notebook, and adapt them in any way you see fit to use in your time management programme.

Happy planning. Congratulations on committing to a successful time management programme.

Term Planning Calendar

Fill in due dates for assignments and essays, dates of tests/exams, and important non-academic activities and events

Month	MONDAY	TUESDAY	WEDNESDAY	THURSDAY	FRIDAY	SATURDAY	SUNDAY

Priority rating	Scheduled?	**Priority Tasks This Week**
		Week beginning ▮▮▮ and ending ▮▮▮

Daily Schedule

date:

Assignments Due

To Do/Errands

Homework

Schedule

5
6
7
8
9
10
11
12
1
2
3
4
5
6
7
8
9
10
11
12

Index